Nelson Phonics 1

First Year of School

Simarjeet K Dhaliwal and Melanie Porter

THOMSON
NELSON

Australia · Canada · Mexico · New Zealand · Singapore · Spain · United Kingdom · United States

THOMSON
NELSON

Nelson Phonics is published by Thomson Learning Australia and distributed as follows:

AUSTRALIA	NEW ZEALAND	CANADA
Level 7, 80 Dorcas Street	Unit 4B, Rosedale Office Park	1120 Birchmount Road
South Melbourne 3205	331 Rosedale Road	Toronto, ON M1K 5G4
Victoria	Albany, North Shore 0632	

First published in 2007
10 9 8 7 6 5 4 3 2 1
11 10 09 08 07

Text © 2007 Nelson Australia Pty Ltd
Illustrations © 2007 Nelson Australia Pty Ltd

Copyright
Apart from fair dealing for the purposes of study, research, criticism or review, or as permitted under Part VB of the Copyright Act, no part of this book may be reproduced by any process without permission. Copyright owners may take legal action against a person who infringes their copyright through unauthorised copying. Enquiries should be directed to the publisher.

Nelson Phonics 1: First Year of School
ISBN-10 0 17 013106 8
ISBN-13 978 0 17 013106 3

Text by Simarjeet K Dhaliwal and Melanie Porter
Illustrations by Dee Texidor
Edited by Daniel Aspinall
Publishing Editor Rosanna Morales
Designed by Karen Mayo and Mandi Cole
Production Controller Kirstin Boshier
Printed by Ligare Book Printers

This title is published under the imprint of Thomson Nelson.
Nelson Australia Pty Ltd ACN 058 280 149 (incorporated in Victoria) trading as Thomson Learning Australia.

Email nelson@thomsonlearning.com.au
Website www.thomsonlearning.com.au

Contents

Introduction
- Using *Nelson Phonics 1* iv
- Scope and Sequence of *Nelson Phonics 1* v

Unit 1
- Syllables 2
- Rhyme 5

Unit 2
- Ss 8
- Mm 10
- Tt 12
- Ff 14
- Aa 16
- Review 17

Unit 3
- Rr 19
- Dd 20
- Gg 22
- Oo 24
- Ii 25
- Review 26

Unit 4
- Ll 28
- Pp 30
- Uu 32
- Hh 33
- Cc 34
- Review 35

Unit 5
- Ee 37
- Bb 38
- Nn 40
- Kk; ck 42
- Vv 44
- Review 46

Unit 6
- Ww 48
- Jj 49
- Yy 50
- Xx 51
- Qu 52
- Review 53

Unit 7
- Zz 54
- Th 55
- Sh 56
- Ch 58
- Review 60

Introduction

Nelson Phonics 1 addresses the four essential skills children need in order to read and spell. These include:
- phonological awareness
- visual (graphological) processing
- letter–sound (phonics) relationships
- spelling.

Phonological awareness is the explicit awareness of the sound structures of spoken language. Training in phonological awareness helps children 'tune in' to the sounds of the English language. Children learn that sentences are made up of words, and that words are made up of separate sounds. They also develop the skills to separate words into sounds, and to blend and manipulate sounds to make new words. Furthermore, children learn how sounds make new words. Phonological awareness includes skills such as rhyming, segmenting syllables and identifying and manipulating the sounds in words. It is an important prerequisite for developing literacy, and can even be used to predict a child's success at learning how to read and spell.

Phonics is the understanding of the relationship between the letters of the alphabet and the individual sounds in the English language. While there are only 26 letters in the alphabet, there are 44 sounds in spoken English. Children learn that individual sounds are represented by different letter combinations.

The *Nelson Phonics* Workbooks focus on phonological awareness and phonics. Research shows that phonological awareness and sound–letter relationships (phonics) are the most important foundation skills for a beginner reader. Simultaneous focus on both skills increases the child's success in acquiring early literacy skills.

Using *Nelson Phonics 1*

Nelson Phonics 1 should be used as part of the classroom literacy program for children at a beginner stage of literacy development. Parents can also support their child's literacy development by using this Workbook at home.

Nelson Phonics 1 introduces beginner readers to the phonological awareness skills of **syllabification** and **rhyme**, then introduces **individual sounds**.

The activities require children to:
- listen for the target sound in spoken words
- visually recognise the letter that represents that sound
- write the letter that represents the target sound.

This Workbook adopts a multi-sensory approach to teaching children about sounds and letters. This approach includes *seeing, listening, feeling* and *writing* sounds, letters and words. Multi-sensory learning has been shown to cater for the learning styles of a greater range of children.

Icons are used in the activity instructions to help children understand what is required in each task. The key for these icons is as follows:

Clap the syllables.

Say the sound or name the picture.

- Listen.
- Draw or colour the picture.
- Circle the picture.
- Draw a line.
- Cross out the picture.
- Trace with your finger.
- Trace the letter with your pencil.
- Write the letter.
- Change the words.

Scope and Sequence of *Nelson Phonics 1*

Nelson Phonics 1 has 7 units. Unit 1 focuses on children's ability to work with the syllables within words and to identify words that rhyme. Units 2 to 7 focus on the consonant and short vowel sounds found in the alphabet. The common digraphs 'sh', 'ch' and 'th', which are produced as one sound, are also included.

Individual sounds in each unit have been grouped based on how often they occur in language, how different they are from other sounds, and according to a sequence widely used by educators and within curricula.

The main goal of teaching beginner readers phonological awareness skills is to develop their ability to listen for individual sounds. In the *Nelson Phonics* Workbooks, children are expected to name the pictures and listen for the sounds in the words they say. They will therefore benefit from naming the pictures with an adult before completing the activities. This will ensure that they understand the pictured vocabulary.

Each unit concludes with a Unit Review, in which children apply their knowledge of the sounds addressed in current and previous units. A child's ability to complete the Unit Review activities will provide feedback on the progress of individual children and inform future teaching strategies.

The *Nelson Phonics* CD-ROM contains a Teacher's Guide with key teaching points and activity ideas, as well as a range of interactive activities for use across the three year levels. The interactive activities on the CD-ROM are presented in three sections:

- Teaching Objects (for whole-class learning)
- Learning Objects (for independent or group learning)
- Task Review (for teacher–student evaluation).

These activities have been specially designed to consolidate and extend on the topics covered in the Workbooks.

Syllables

Name the pictures in each box. Say the words together to make a longer word.

Draw a line to match the word they make.

earring

football

cowboy

rainbow

sandwich

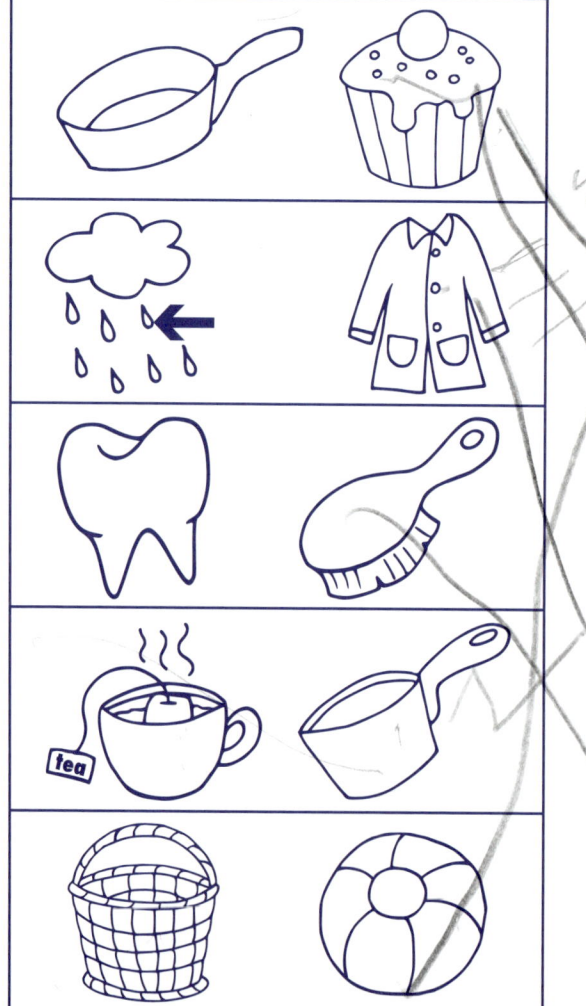

basketball

pancake

teapot

raincoat

toothbrush

Unit 1 Syllables and Rhyme

2

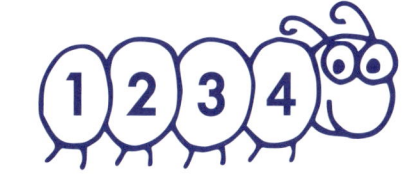

Syllables

Clap the syllables in the word.

Colour a hand for each clap.

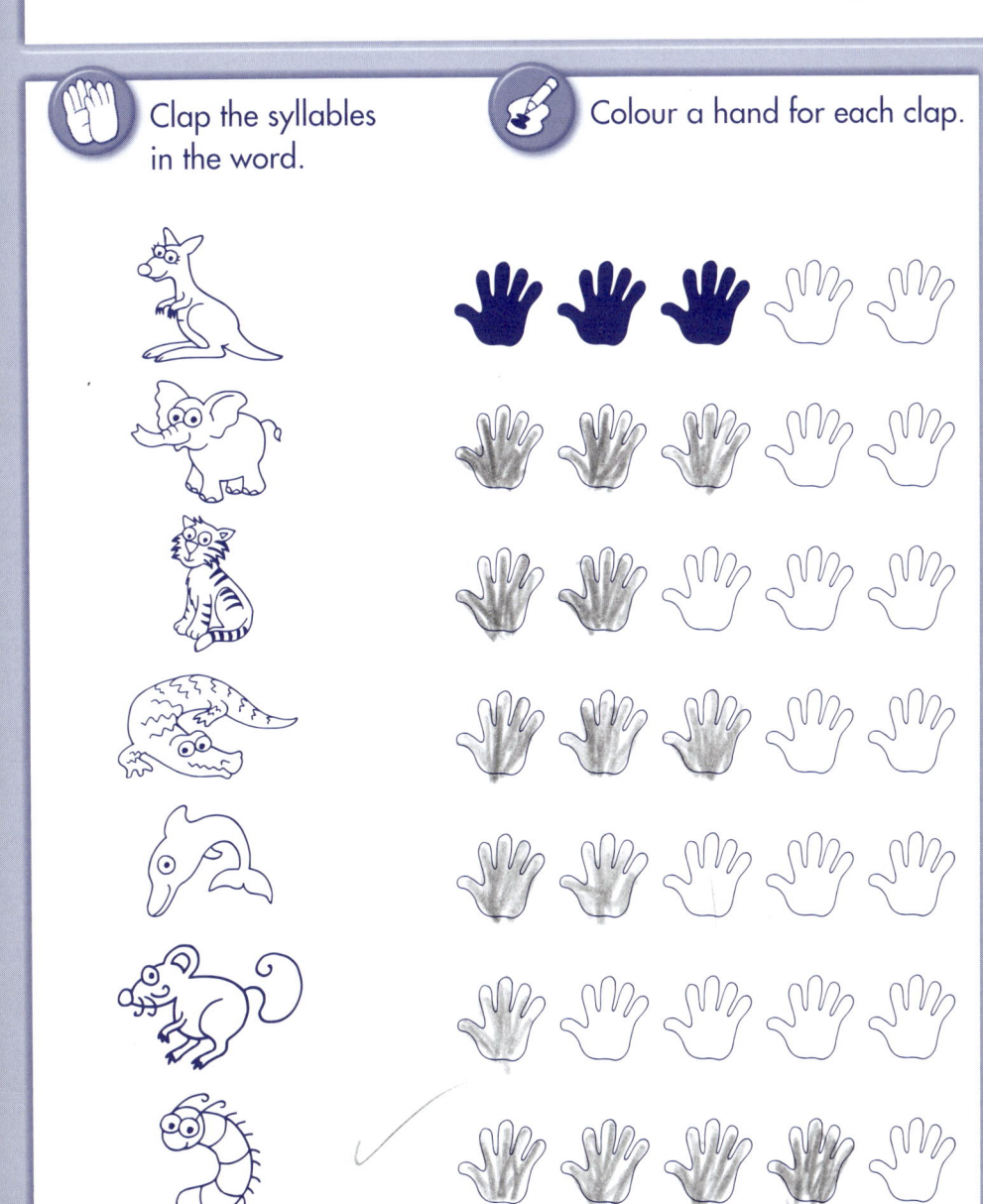

Clap the syllables in each word.

Draw a line to the number of syllables you hear in each word.

Unit 1 Syllables and Rhyme

Syllables

Listen for the syllable that sounds the same in both words.

Draw a line to the picture that shows the syllable the words share.

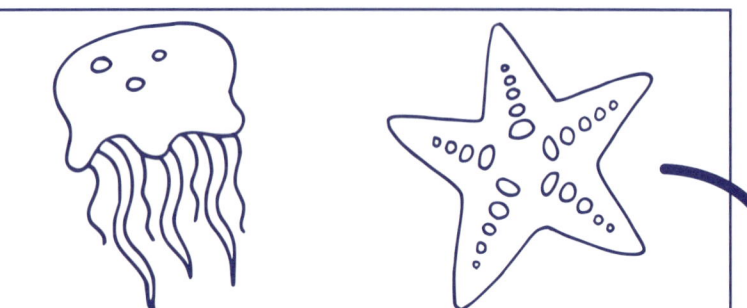

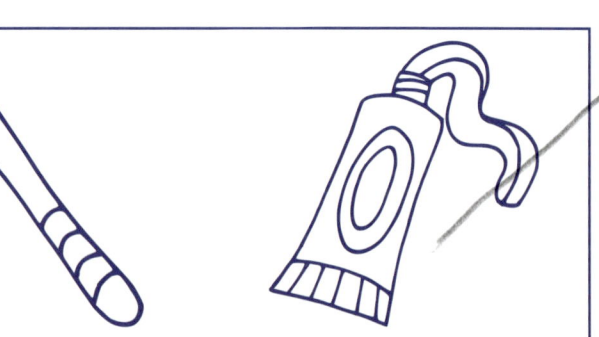

sand 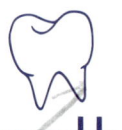
tooth 
water 
ball 
fish 
ring

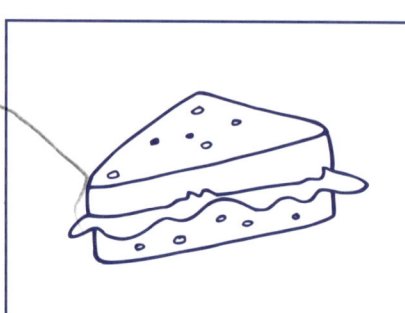

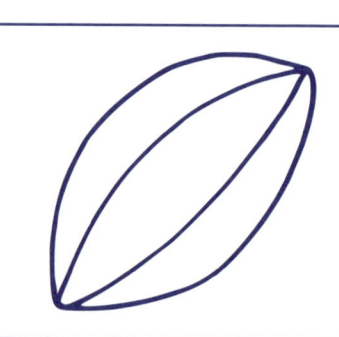

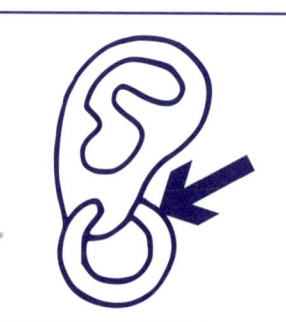

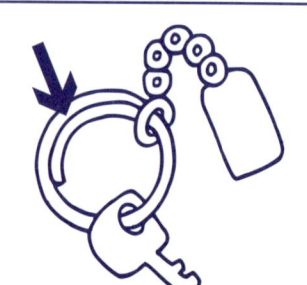

Unit 1 Syllables and Rhyme

4

Rhyme

Name the pictures. Finish drawing the pictures that rhyme.

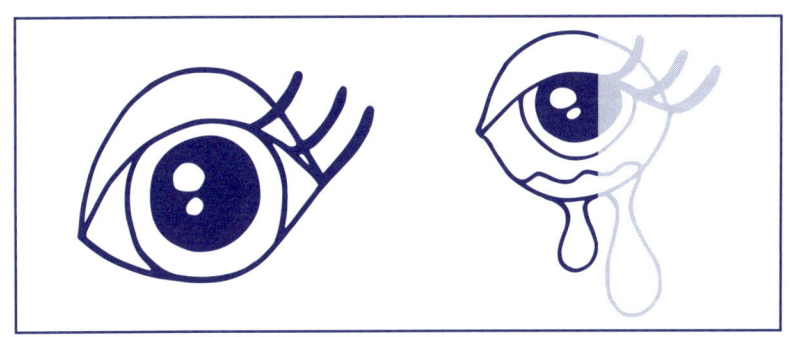

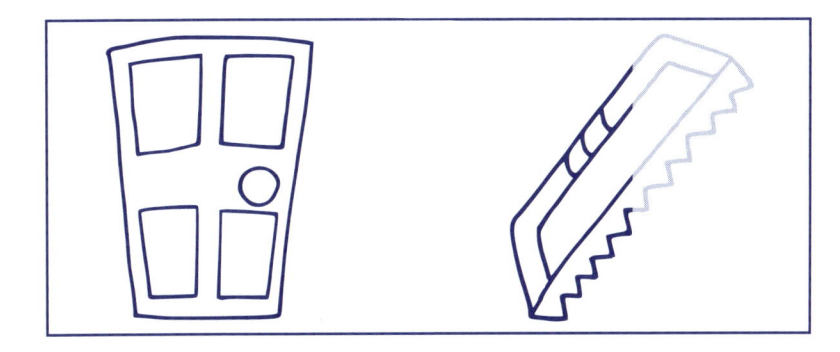

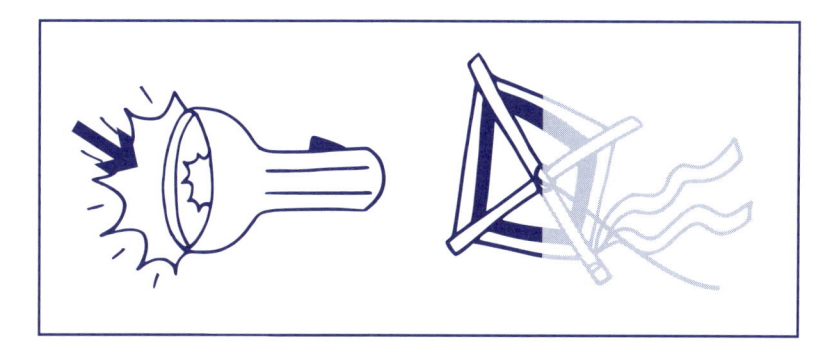

Rhyme

Draw a line between the pictures that rhyme.

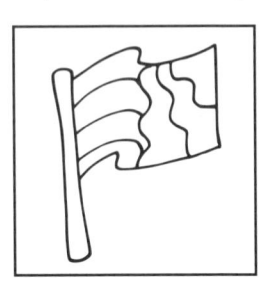

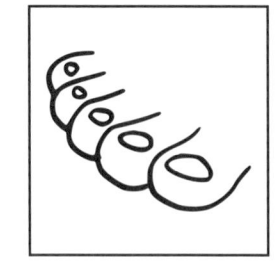

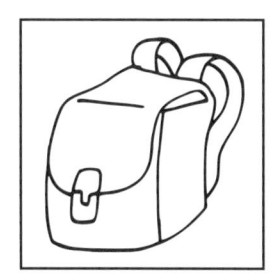

Draw your own rhyming words.

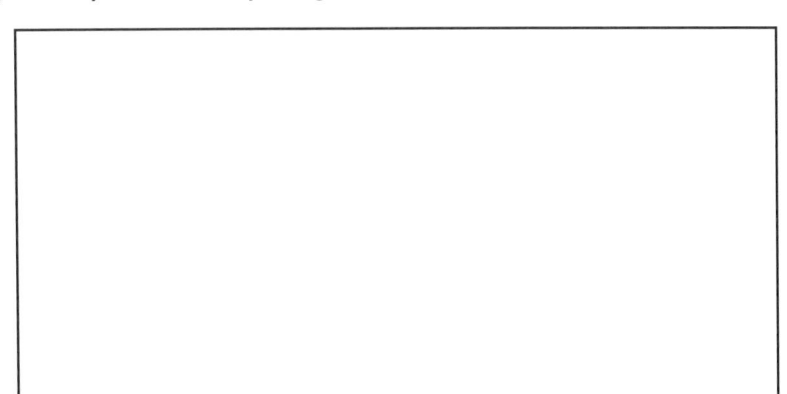

Rhyme

Circle the picture in each box that does not rhyme.

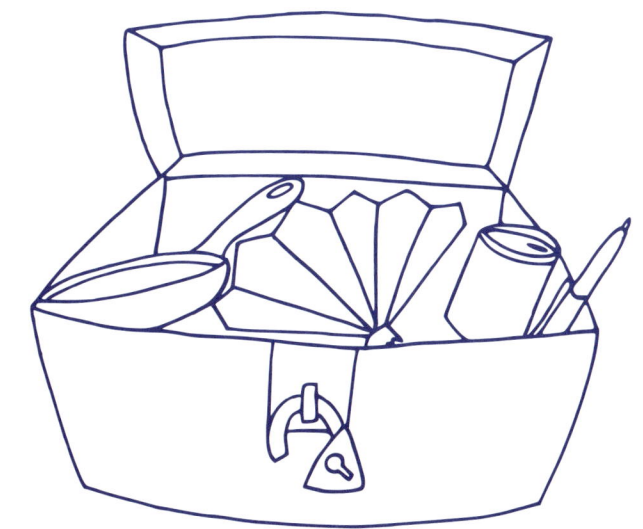

Unit 1 Syllables and Rhyme

7

Ss

Trace the letters with your finger. **Say the sound.** **Trace the letters.**

S s S s S s

Name the pictures. **Colour the pictures that start with the 's' sound.**

Circle the pictures that start with 's'.

Unit 2 s

8

Name the pictures. Cross the picture in each row that **does not** end in the 's' sound.

Find all the things that end with the 's' sound. Draw a line to the suitcase.

Write the missing letter in each word.

_un    _ock    bu_    hor_e

Unit 2   s

Mm

m m m m m m

Trace the letters with your finger. **Say the sound.** **Trace the letters.**

Name the pictures. **Colour the pictures that start with the 'm' sound.**

Name the pictures in each row. **Cross the picture in each row that does not start with the 'm' sound.**

Unit 2 m

Name all the things you see in the picture.

Circle the pictures that end with the 'm' sound.

Colour both pictures in each box if they end with the 'm' sound.

Write the missing letter in each word.

_at    _ap    ja_    ra_

Unit 2   m

Tt

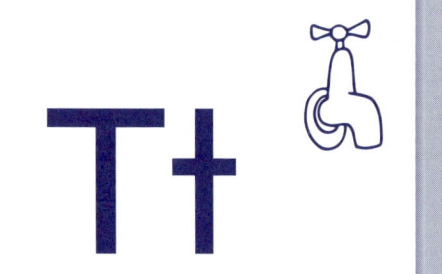

Trace the letters with your finger. **Say the sound.** **Trace the letters.**

t t t t t t

Name the pictures. **Colour the pictures that start with the 't' sound.**

Find 5 pictures that start with the 't' sound. Draw a line to each toe.

Unit 2   t

12

Name the pictures in each row.

Cross the picture in each row that **does not** end with the 't' sound.

Colour the pictures that end with the 't' sound.

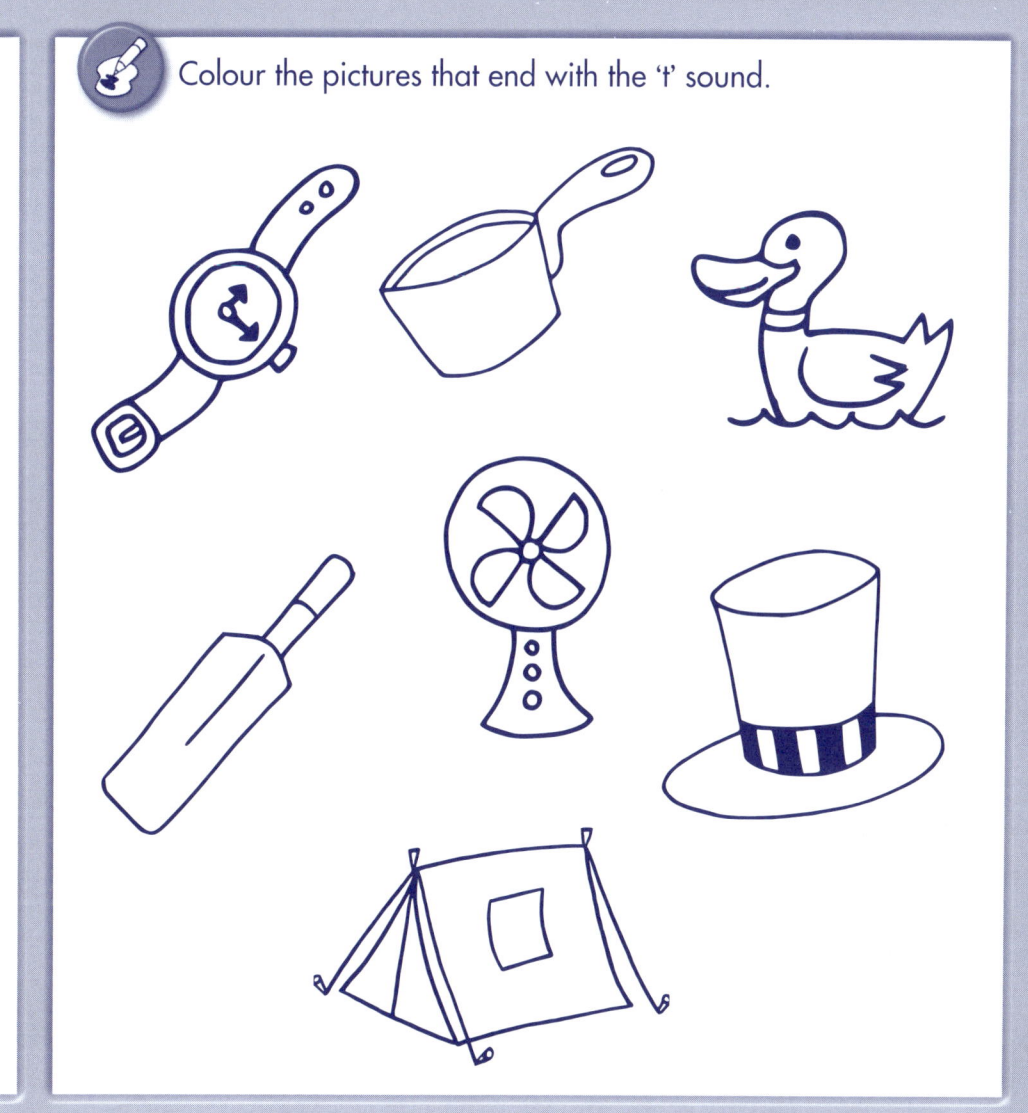

Write the missing letter in each word.

_ap  _en  ha_  ca_

Unit 2 t

13

Ff

Trace the letters with your finger. **Say the sound.** **Trace the letters.**

f f f f f f

Name the pictures. **Colour the pictures that start with the 'f' sound.**

Name the pictures in each row. **Cross the picture in each row that does not start with the 'f' sound.**

Unit 2   f

14

Name the pictures.

Circle the pictures that have the 'f' sound at the end.

Draw a line from the clown's hand to the balloons showing pictures that end with the 'f' sound.

Write the missing letter in each word.

_an    _ire    lea_    scar_

Unit 2 f

15

Aa

a a a a a a a

Trace the letters with your finger. **Say the sound.** **Trace the letters.**

Name the pictures. Colour the pictures that have the 'a' sound in the middle.

Colour the pictures that have the 'a' sound in the middle.

Write the missing letter in each word.

f_n   b_t   c_t

Unit 2   a

16

Unit 2 Review

s m t f a

Name the pictures. Write the missing letters.

ha_

_ _t

f_ _

Change the first word into the second word.

hat  to _ _ _

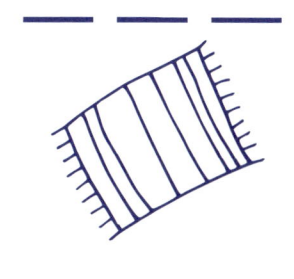

cat to _ _ _

Trace the letters that are underlined.

The <u>f</u>at c<u>a</u>t <u>s</u>at on the ma<u>t</u>.

Unit 2 Review

Write the missing letters.

_ock 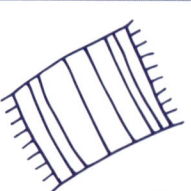 _at  ca_  _ish

Name the picture. **Circle the first sound you hear.**

s / m / t / a

t / f / m / s

Circle the pictures that rhyme with 'cat'.

Name the picture. **Circle the last sound you hear.**

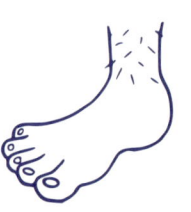

f / t / f / s

m / a / m / s

Write the missing letters.

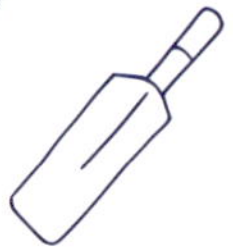

b  _ _   r _ _   j _ _

Rr

Trace the letters with your finger. **Say the sound.** **Trace the letters.**

r r r r r r r

Name the pictures. **Colour the pictures that start with the 'r' sound.**

Colour the rockets that show pictures that start with the 'r' sound.

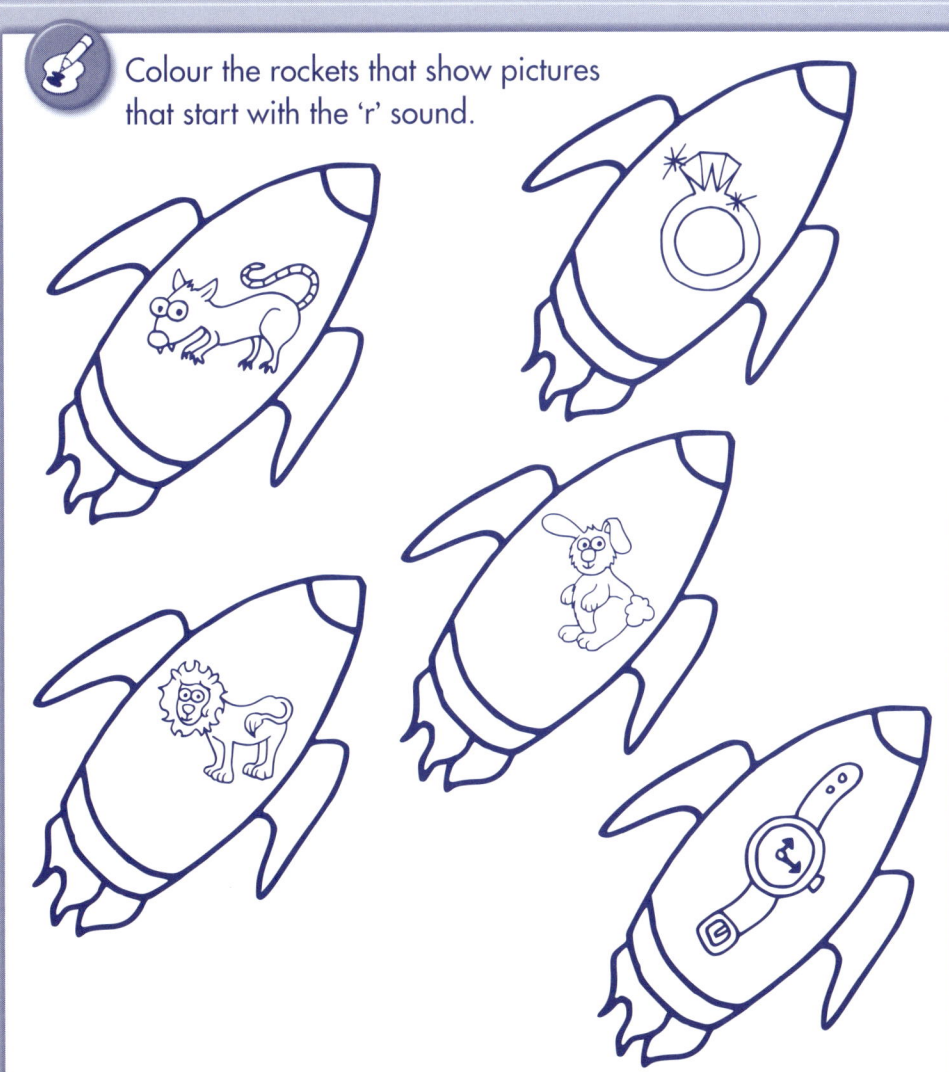

Write the missing letter in each word.

_at   _ain   _ing

Unit 3

Dd

Trace the letters with your finger. **Say the sound.** **Trace the letters.**

d d d d d d

Name the pictures. **Colour the pictures that start with the 'd' sound.**

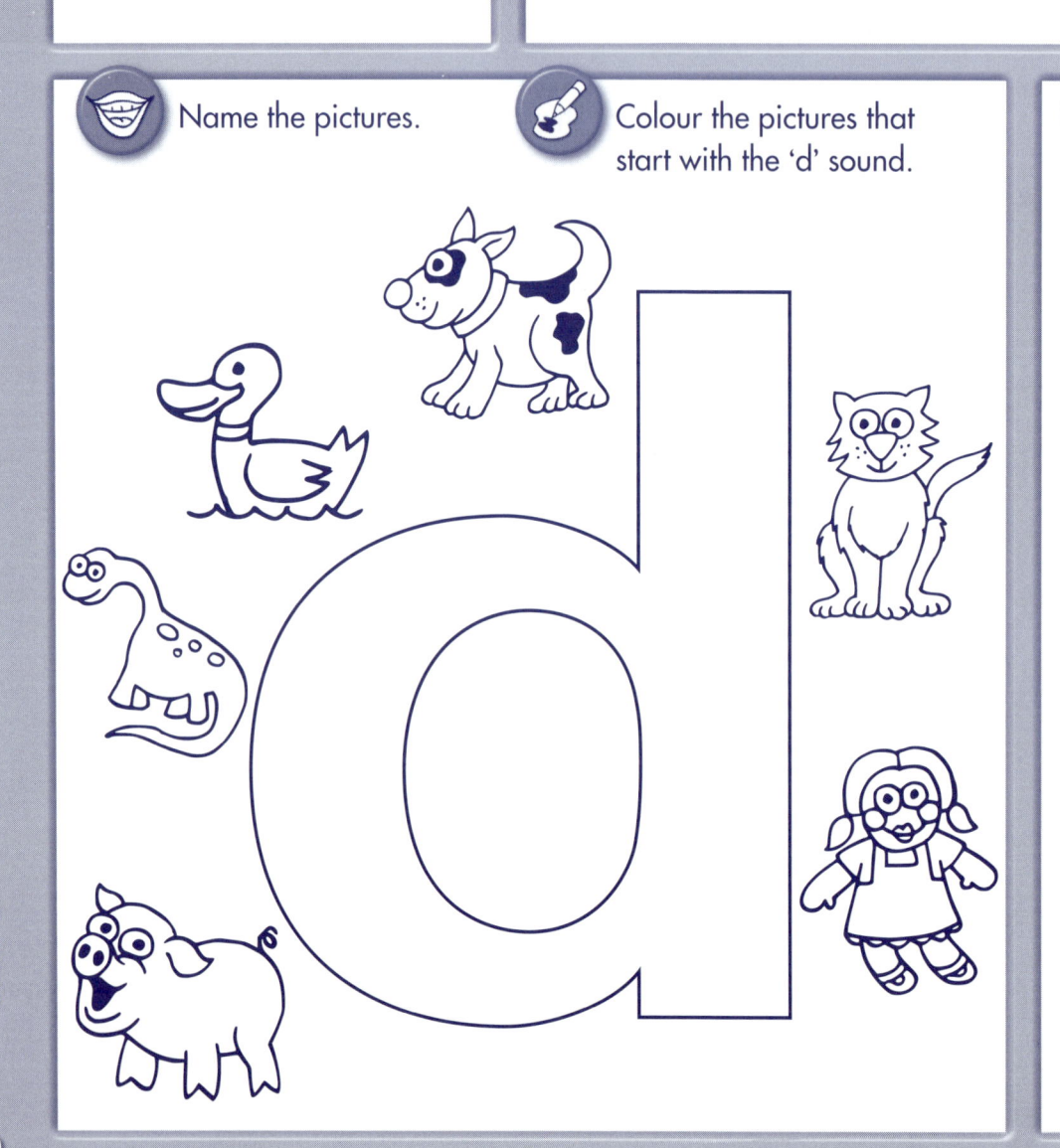

Name the pictures in each row. **Cross the picture in each row that does not start with the 'd' sound.**

Unit 3   d

Name all the things you see in the picture.

Circle the pictures that end in the 'd' sound.

Colour both pictures in each row if they end with the 'd' sound.

Write the missing letter in each word.

_og    _uck    be_    sa_

Unit 3   d

21

Gg

g g g g g g g

Trace the letters with your finger. **Say the sound.** **Trace the letters.**

Name the pictures. **Colour the pictures that start with the 'g' sound.**

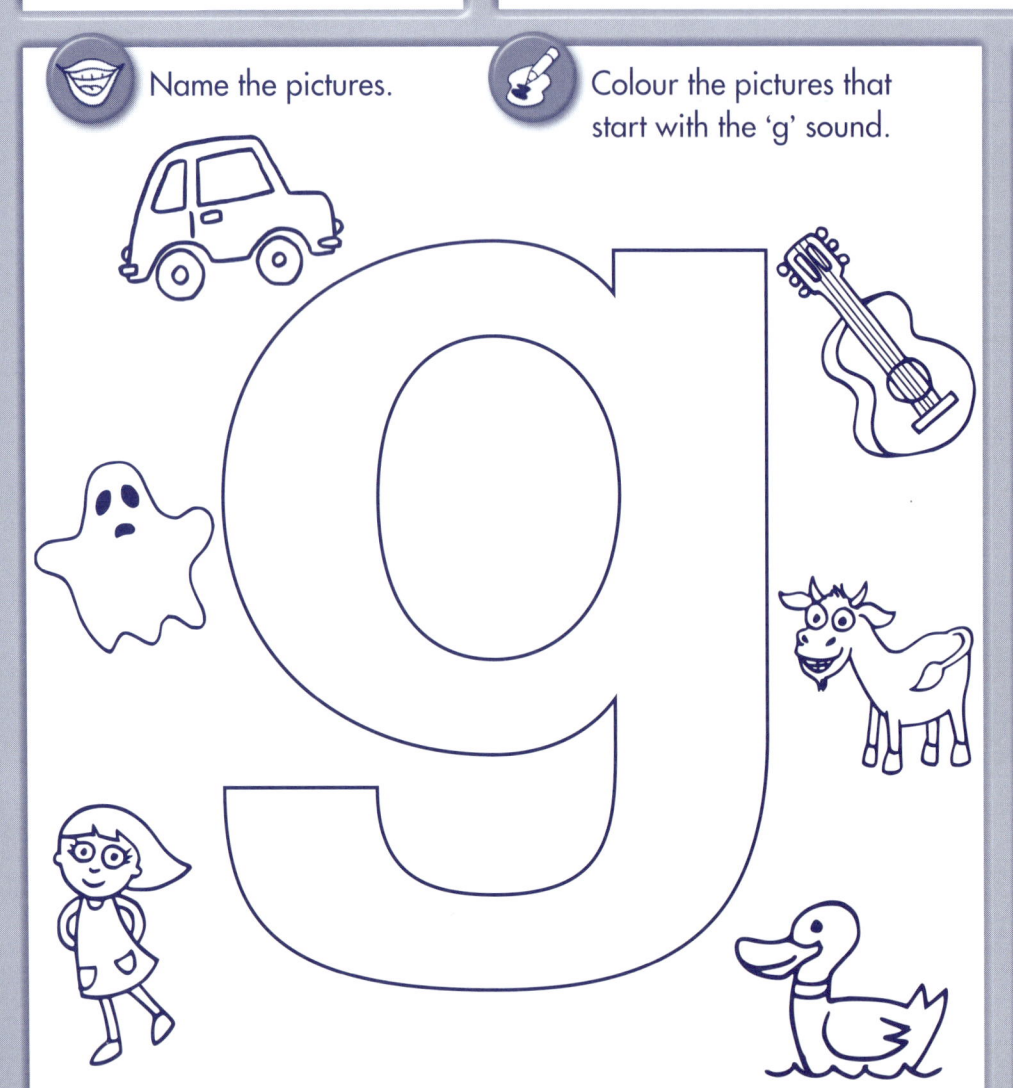

Cross the flowers that show pictures that do not start with the 'g' sound.

Unit 3 g

22

Name all the things you see in the picture.

Circle the pictures that end with the 'g' sound.

Find the pictures that end with the 'g' sound. Draw a line to the log.

Write the missing letter in each word.

_irl    _oat    ba_    pi_

Unit 3   g

23

Oo

Trace the letters with your finger. **Say the sound.** **Trace the letters.**

Name the pictures. **Colour the pictures that have the 'o' sound in the middle.**

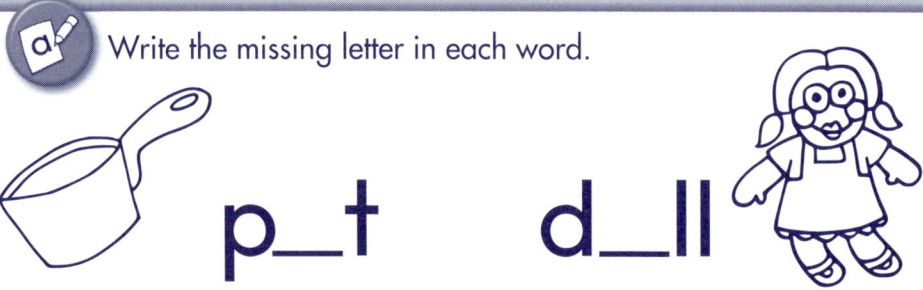

Circle the pictures in each row that have the same middle sound.

Write the missing letter in each word.

p_t   d_ll

I i

Trace the letters with your finger. Say the sound. Trace the letters.

i i i i i i

Name the pictures. Colour the pictures that have the 'i' sound in the middle.

Cross the picture in each row that **does not** have the same middle sound.

Write the missing letter in each word.

p_g   sh_p

Unit 3   i

Unit 3 Review

r d g o i

Name the pictures. Write the missing letters.

___ _ag t___

_a_ _i_ ___t

Listen to the sound at the end of each word. Write the letter in the box.

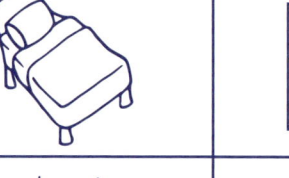

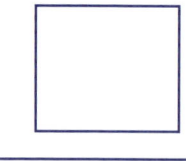

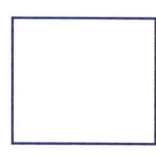

		d

Trace the letters that are underlined.

The sad dog drew a dot on the tag.

Unit 3 Review

Write the missing letters.

_ose    _oor    le_    d_ll    b_n

Name the picture.

Circle the first sound you hear.

g	d
o	g
g	i
r	o

Circle the pictures that rhyme with 'rose'.

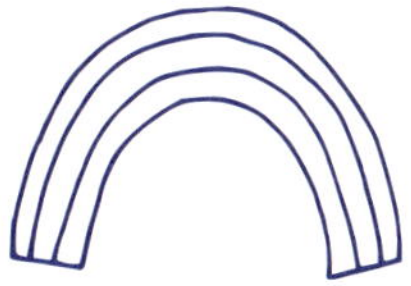

Name the picture.

Circle the middle sound you hear.

i	o
d	g
g	r
o	i

Circle the pictures that rhyme with 'dig'.

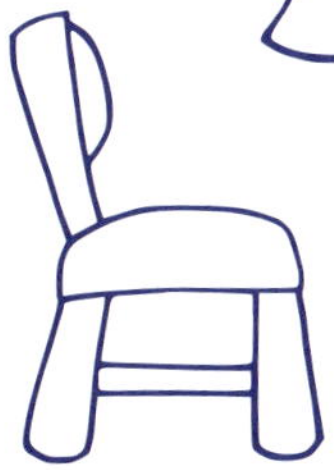

Unit 3   Review – r, d, g, o, i

27

Ll

Trace the letters with your finger. Say the sound. Trace the letters.

l l l l l l

Name the pictures. Colour the pictures that start with the 'l' sound.

Draw a line to the lion from each drumstick that shows a picture that starts with the 'l' sound.

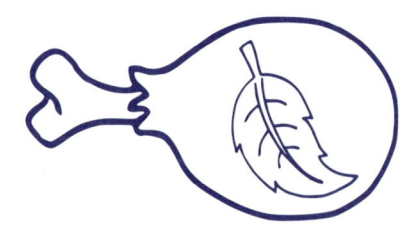

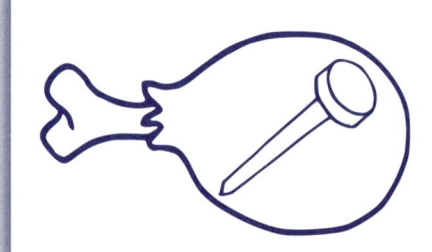

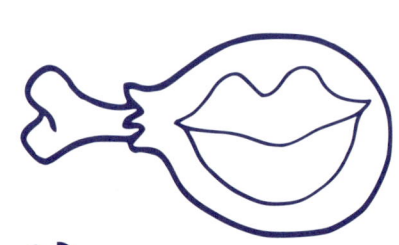

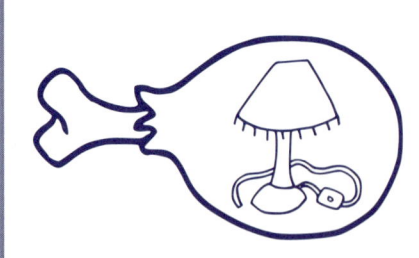

Unit 4 l

28

Cross the picture in each row that **does not** end with the same sound.

Help the snail reach the end. Circle the pictures along the way that end with the 'l' sound.

Write the missing letter in each word.

_ook    _ove    snai_    gir_

Unit 4

29

P p

Trace the letters with your finger. **Say the sound.** **Trace the letters.**

p p p p p p

Name the pictures. **Colour the pictures that start with the 'p' sound.**

Colour the pictures that start with the 'p' sound.

Unit 4 P

30

Cross the picture in each row that **does not** end with the 'p' sound.

Draw a line from the ship to all the pictures that end with the 'p' sound.

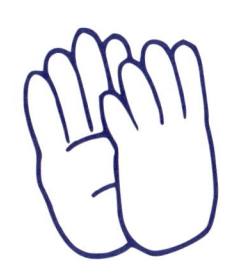

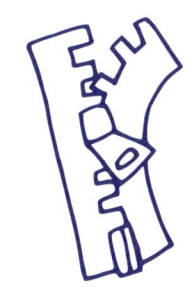

Write the missing letter in each word.

_ig    _aint    mo_    cu_

Unit 4 P

31

Uu

Trace the letters with your finger. **Say the sound.** **Trace the letters.**

u u u u u u u

Name the pictures. **Colour the pictures that have the 'u' sound in the middle.**

Circle the pictures that have the same middle sound as 'cup'.

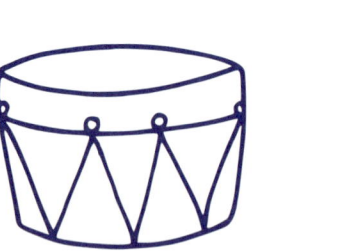

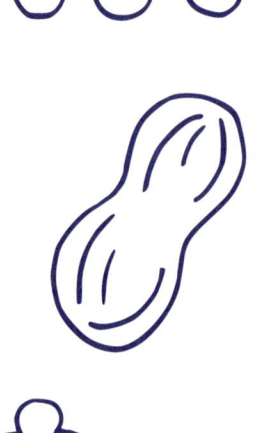

Write the missing letter in each word.

c_p    b_g

Hh

Trace the letters with your finger. **Say the sound.** **Trace the letters.**

h h h h h h

Colour the pictures that start with the 'h' sound.

Draw a line from the fishing hook to each fish that shows a picture that starts with the 'h' sound.

Write the missing letter in each word.

_at   _orse

Cc

Trace the letters with your finger. **Say the sound.** **Trace the letters.**

c c c c c c c

Name the pictures. **Colour the pictures that start with the 'c' sound.**

Name all the things you see in the picture. **Circle the pictures that start with the 'c' sound.**

Write the missing letter in each word.

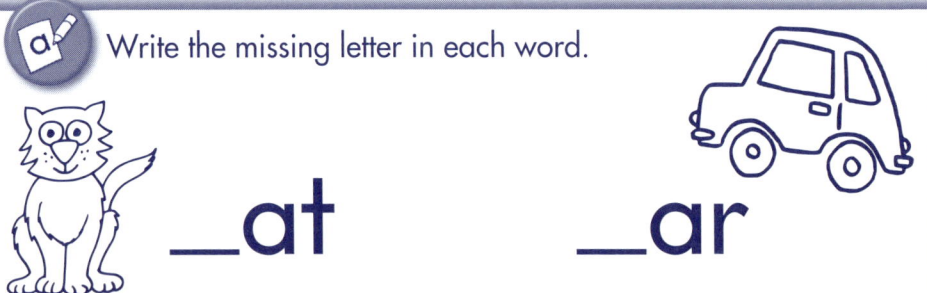

_at   _ar

Unit 4 Review

l p u h c

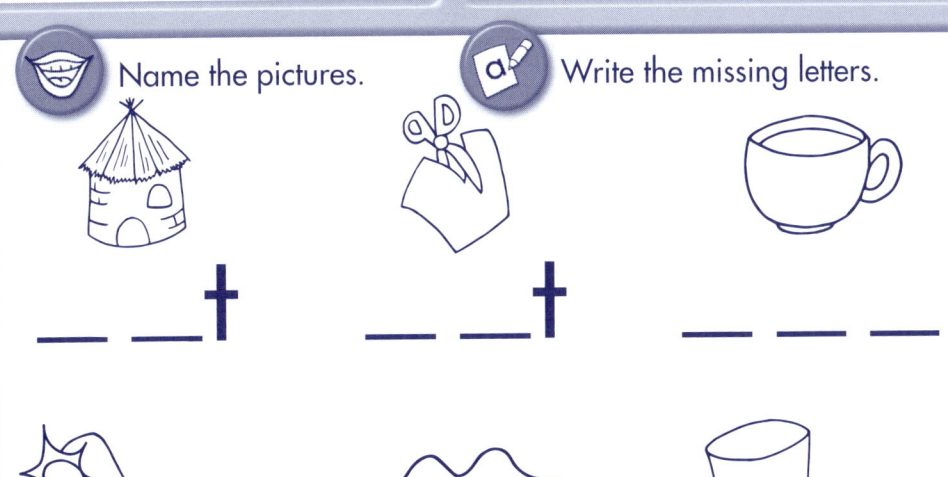

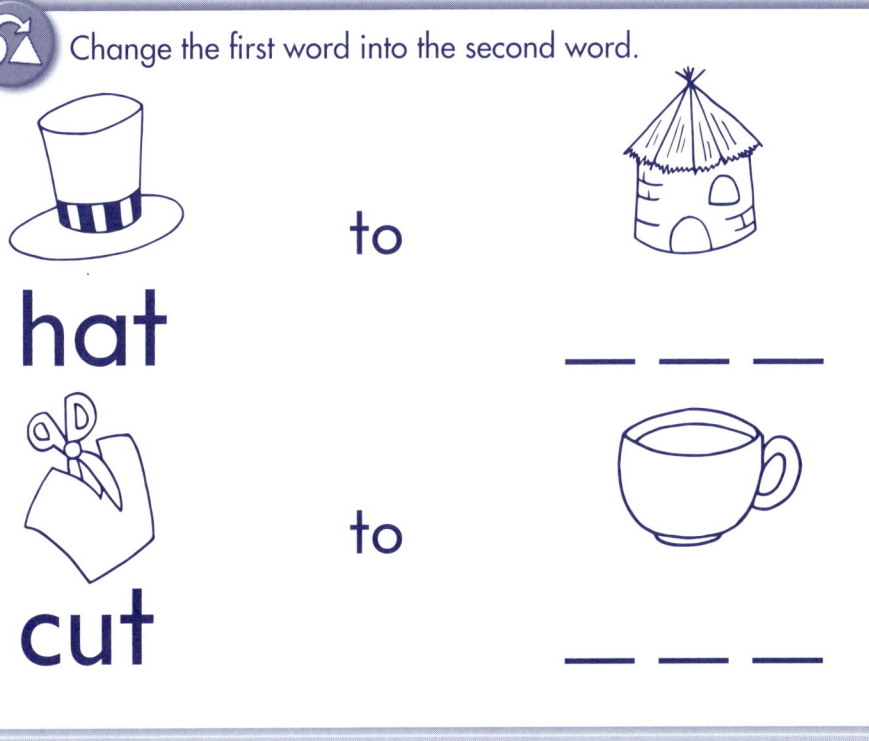

Name the pictures. Write the missing letters.

_ _ t (hut)
_ _ t (cut)
_ _ _ (cup)

_ it (lit)
_ i _ s (lips)
_ at (hat)

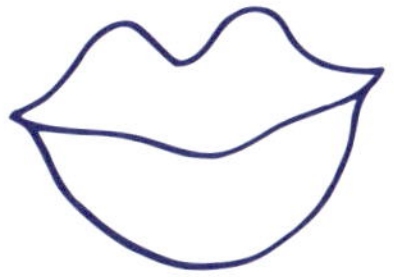

Change the first word into the second word.

hat to _ _ _ (hut)

cut to _ _ _ (cup)

Trace the letters that are underlined.

The boy hit his lip on the cup.

35

Unit 4 Review

Write the missing letters.

_at   _at   b_g   ma_   cur_

Listen to the first sound in the words.

Write the letter in the space under each picture.

Read the word above and circle the picture that matches.

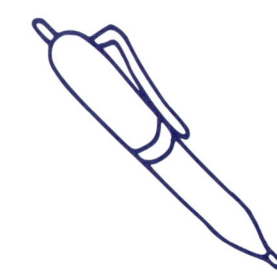

Name the picture. **Circle the first sound you hear.**

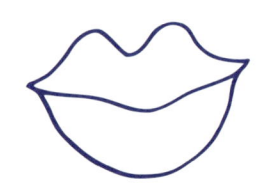

- c / p
- u / h
- h / l
- l / c

Name the picture. **Circle the middle sound you hear.**

- p / l
- h / u

Ee

Trace the letters with your finger. Say the sound. Trace the letters.

e e e e e e e

Name the pictures. Colour the pictures that have the 'e' sound in the middle.

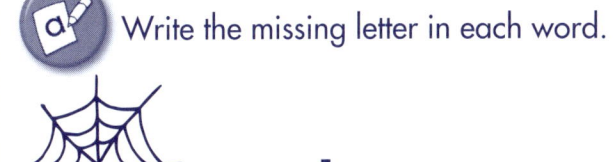

Colour the pillows that show pictures that have the same middle sound as 'bed'.

Write the missing letter in each word.

w_b   p_g

Unit 5 • e

37

Bb

Trace the letters with your finger. **Say the sound.** **Trace the letters.**

b b b b b b

Name the pictures. **Colour the pictures that start with the 'b' sound.**

Name all the things you see in the picture. **Circle the pictures that start with the 'b' sound.**

Unit 5   b

Draw a line to join the pictures that end with the same sound.

Circle the pictures that end with the 'b' sound.

Circle the pictures that end with the same sound as 'web'.

Write the missing letter in each word.

_ed    _all    cra_    we_

Unit 5   b

39

Nn

Trace the letters with your finger. **Say the sound.** **Trace the letters.**

n n n n n n

Name the pictures. **Colour the pictures that start with the 'n' sound.**

Colour the eggs in the nest that show pictures that start with the 'n' sound.

Unit 5 n

40

Colour each picture that ends with the same sound as 'man'.

Name the two pictures in each row.

Colour both pictures in each row if they end with the same sound.

Write the missing letter in each word.

_et    _ut    moo_ 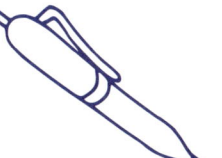   pe_

Unit 5   n

41

Kk

Trace the letters with your finger. **Say the sound.** **Trace the letters.**

k k k k k k

Name the pictures. **Colour the pictures that start with the 'k' sound.**

Cross the picture in each row that does not start with the 'k' sound.

Unit 5   k

42

- Name all the things you see in the picture.
- Circle the things that end with the 'k' sound.

- Say the sound.
- Trace the letters.

ck **ck** ck

tru<u>ck</u> blo<u>ck</u> du<u>ck</u>

so<u>ck</u> lo<u>ck</u> clo<u>ck</u>

Write the missing letter in each word.

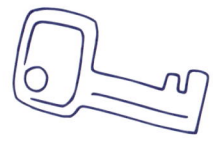

_ey    _ing    ca_e    boo_

Unit 5 k/ck

43

Vv

Trace the letters with your finger. Say the sound. Trace the letters.

v v v v v v v

Name the pictures. Colour the pictures that start with the 'v' sound.

Circle the things that start with the same sound as 'van'.

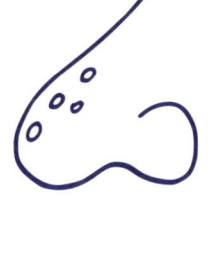

Unit 5   v

44

Trace the 'v' to finish the love heart.

Colour the pictures that end with the 'v' sound.

Draw a line from the pictures that end with the 'v' sound to the beehive.

Write the missing letter in each word.

_an    _ase    lo_e    wa_e

Unit 5   v

45

Unit 5 Review

e b n k/ck v

Name the pictures. Write the missing letters.

m_e_n   h_e_n   s_o_ck

_n_u_t   _v_a_n   _b_i_b

Change the first word into the second word.

pin   to   _p_ _e_ _n_

fan   to   _v_ _a_ _n_

Trace the letters that are underlined.

The m<u>en</u> ha<u>ve</u> a <u>b</u>ig <u>v</u>an.

Unit 5 Review

Write the missing letters.

_a_y    _et    du__    glo_e    b_d

Name the picture.

- b / n
- k / e
- n / v
- v / n

Circle the first sound you hear.

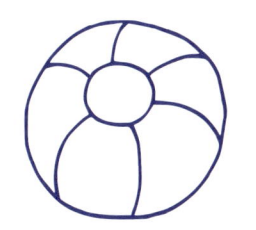

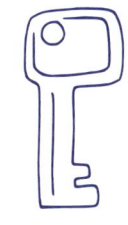

- k / v
- e / n
- v / b
- n / e

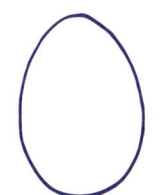

Circle the words that end with the same sound as 'pin'.

Write the letter of the sound in the box.

47

Ww

Trace the letters with your finger. **Say the sound.** **Trace the letters.**

w w w w w w w

Name the pictures.

Colour the pictures that start with the 'w' sound.

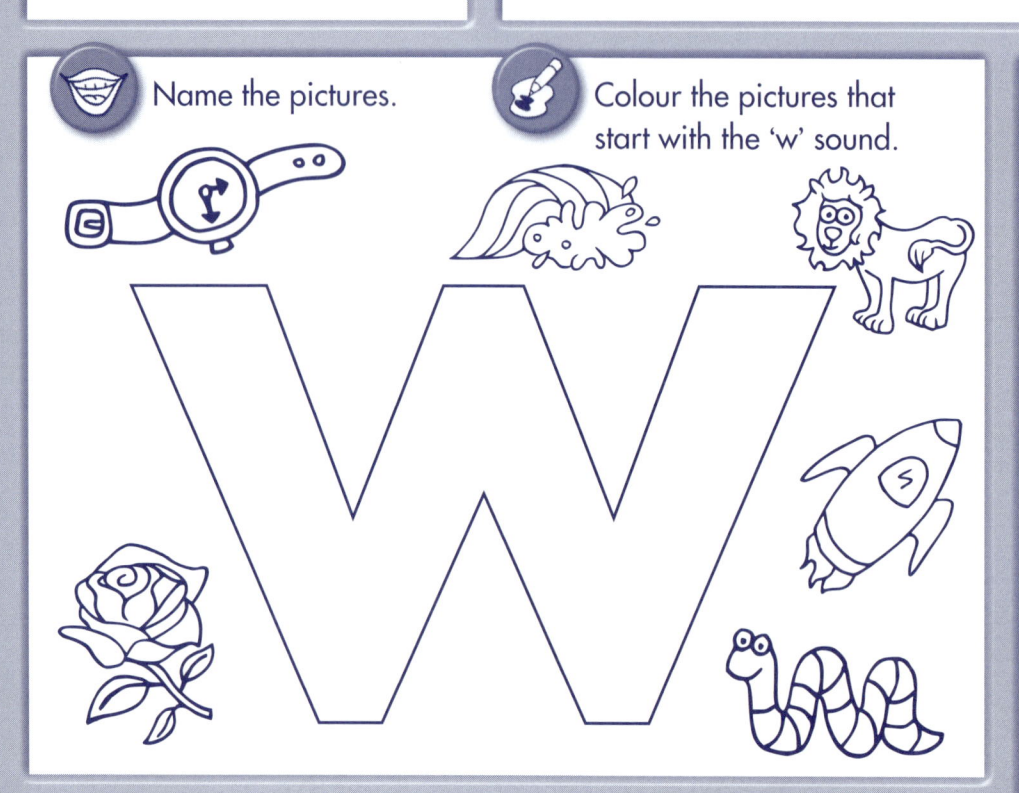

Colour the pictures that start with the same sound as 'web'.

Write the missing letter in each word.

_eb    _ave

Unit 6 w

Jj

Trace the letters with your finger. **Say the sound.** **Trace the letters.**

j J j J j J j j j

Name the pictures. **Colour the pictures that start with the 'j' sound.**

Circle the pictures that start with the same sound as 'jeans'.

Write the missing letter in each word.

_ump   _am

Unit 6 j

49

Yy

Trace the letters with your finger. **Say the sound.** **Trace the letters.**

y y y y y y y

Name the pictures. **Colour the pictures that start with the 'y' sound.**

Draw a line from the yo-yo to each picture that starts with 'y'.

Write the missing letter in each word.

_acht   _awn

Xx

Trace the letters with your finger. **Say the sound.** **Trace the letters.**

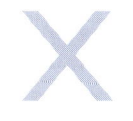

x x x x x x

Name the pictures.

Colour the pictures that have the 'x' sound at the end.

Colour the treasure maps that show a picture that ends with the 'x' sound.

Write the missing letter in each word.

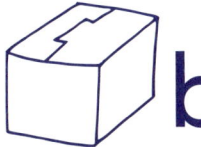

bo_   si_

Unit 6   x

Trace the letters with your finger. Say the sound. Trace the letters.

Qu

qu qu qu qu qu

Name the pictures. Colour the pictures that start with the 'qu' sound.

qu

Colour the pictures that start with the same sound as 'question'.

Write the missing letters in each word.

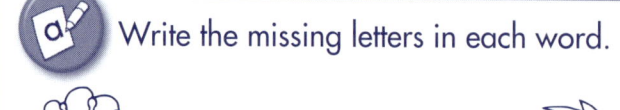

_ _een    _ _iet

Unit 6 qu

52

Unit 6 Review

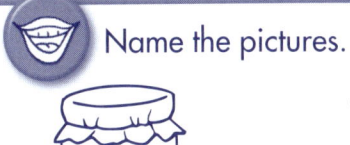

w j y x qu

Name the pictures. Write the missing letters.

_a_ _u_ s_ _

_ _g _ _t _ _een

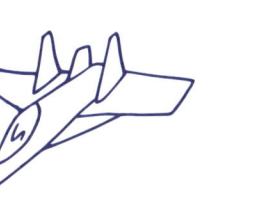

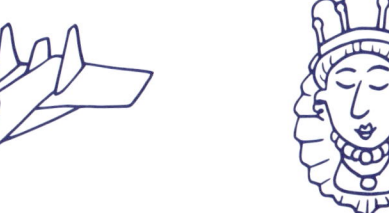

Change the first word into the second word.

sad to _ _ _

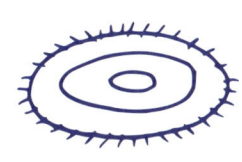

rug to _ _ _

Trace the letters that are underlined.

Grandma pours jam on her wig.

Zz

Trace the letters with your finger. **Say the sound.** **Trace the letters.**

z z z z z z

Name the pictures. **Colour the pictures that start with the 'z' sound.**

Help zebra find the zoo. Trace over the zig-zag trail. **Colour the pictures that start or end with the 'z' sound as you go.**

Write the missing letter in each word.

_ip   bu_z

Unit 7

Th

Trace the letters with your finger. **Say the sound.** **Trace the letters.**

th th th th th th

Name the pictures. **Colour the pictures that start with the 'th' sound.**

Help the boy think of words that start with the 'th' sound. Colour the pictures that start with the same sound as 'think'.

Write the 'th' in each word. **Say the words.**

__is __at __ey

Unit 7 th

Sh

Trace the letters with your finger. Say the sound. Trace the letters.

sh sh sh sh sh sh

Name the pictures. Colour the pictures that start with the 'sh' sound.

Colour the pictures that start with the same sound as 'shark'.

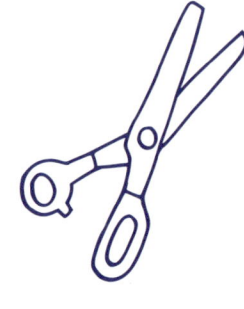

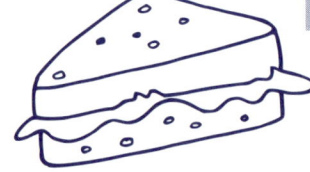

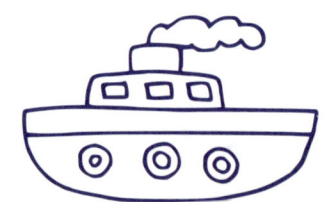

Unit 7   sh

56

Draw a line to join the pictures that end with the same sound.

Circle the 'sh' sound in each word.

Write 'sh' next to each noisy baby to make them quiet.

brush

fish

splash

wash

Write the missing letters in each word.

___oe    ___ell    fi___    bru___

Unit 7 sh

57

Ch

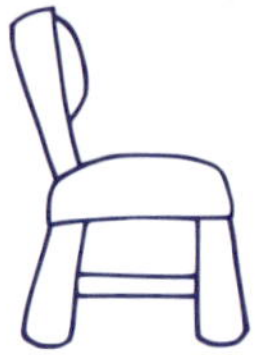

Trace the letters with your finger. **Say the sound.** **Trace the letters.**

ch ch ch ch ch ch

Name the pictures. **Colour the pictures that start with the 'ch' sound.**

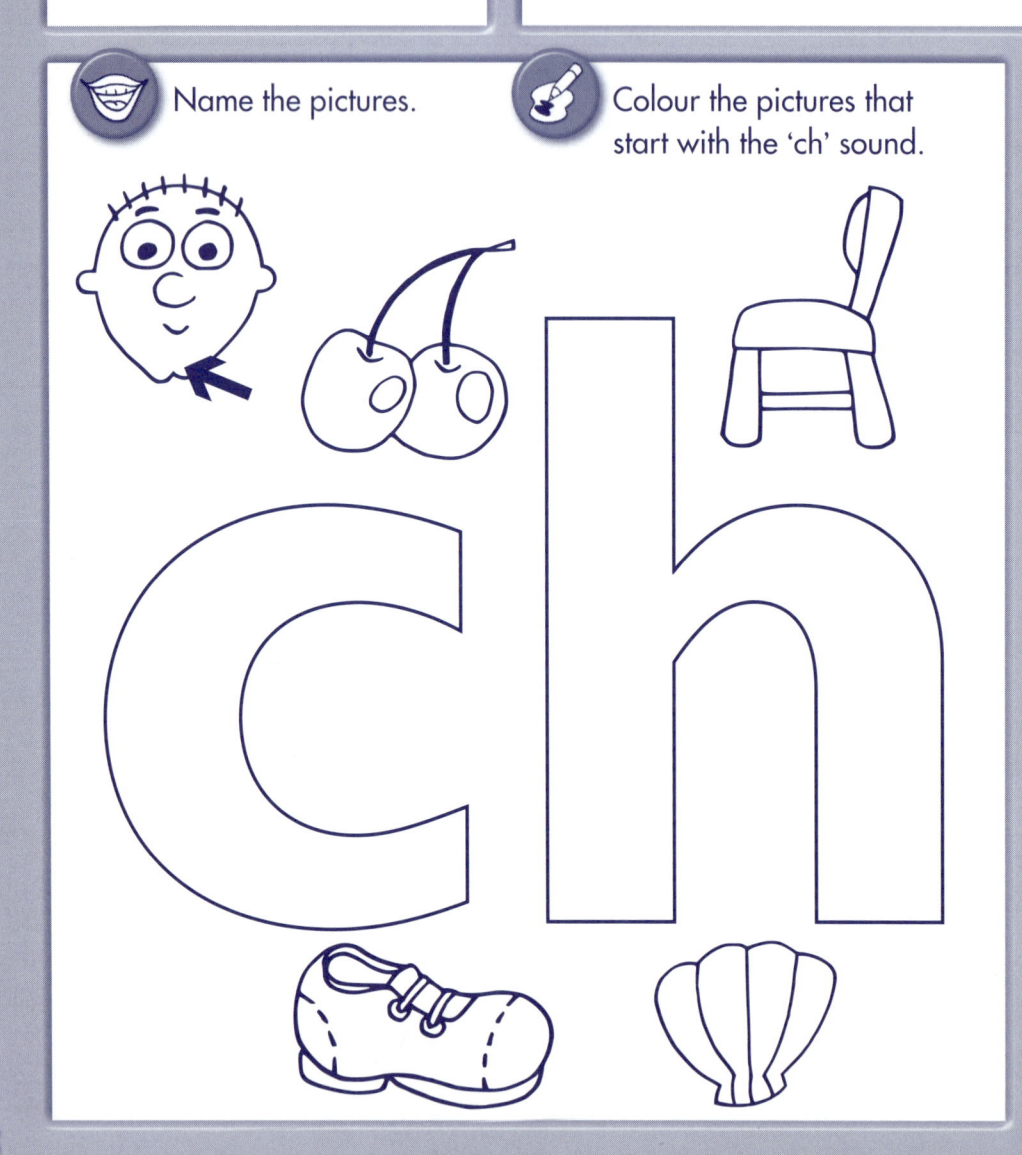

Colour the pictures that start with the same sound as 'cheese'.

Unit 7 ch

58

Colour the pictures if they end with the same sound as 'witch'.

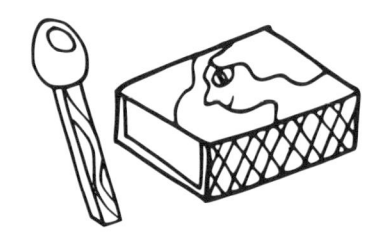

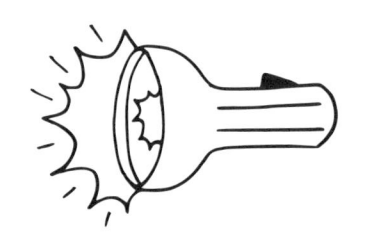

Colour the pictures in each row if they both end with the 'ch' sound.

Write the missing letters in each word.

___air    ___in    tor___    wat___

Unit 7   ch

Unit 7 Review

z   th   ch   sh

Name the pictures. Write the missing letters.

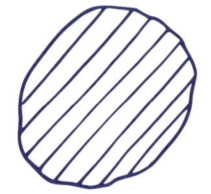

___ip

___i___

___ ___ ___

Change the first word into the second word.

zip to ___ ___ ___

fin to ___ ___ ___

Trace the letters that are underlined.

The zips and chips are on the ship.